Bremen

Bremen – Innenstadt, umgeben von Weser und Wallanlagen.

Bremen – the city centre surrounded by the Weser and the city fortifications.

Jochen Mönch
Hermann Gutmann

# Bremen

## Bremerhaven · Fischerhude · Worpswede

Mit 498 Abbildungen

Edition Temmen

Ein Dorf mit Straßenbahn, nennen die Bremer schmunzelnd, doch mit unverhohlener Liebe, ihre Stadt.

Nun ist Bremen tatsächlich eine Großstadt, Hauptstadt des Bundeslandes Bremen. Doch im Zentrum überragen die Domtürme – wie in alten Zeiten – immer noch die Wohn- und Geschäftshäuser.

Bremen ist die Stadt der kurzen Wege. Man ist überall gleich da. Wer es eilig hat, fährt mit dem Fahrrad oder setzt sich in die Straßenbahn, um – zum Beispiel Freunde vom Flughafen abzuholen.

Um ein Bild der Lage der Stadt und des Landes zu vermitteln, können wir Ihnen sagen, dass die Stadt Bremen auf 53° 4′ 15″ nördlicher Breite und 8° 48′ 15″ östlicher Länge liegt. Genauer geht's nicht.

Festgelegt wurde dieser geographische Punkt auf dem Turm der Ansgariikirche. Die Kirche gibt es nicht mehr, aber der geographische Punkt muss noch da sein. Vermutlich liegt er breit getreten auf dem Fußboden eines Ladengeschäftes, dort, wo einmal die Kirche gestanden hat. Sie können ihn ja mal suchen.

Lebensader des Landes ist die Weser.

Am Übergang von Mittel- zu Unterweser (beim Weserwehr) liegt die Freie Hansestadt Bremen inmitten ihrer niedersächsischen Umgebung. Doch Landesgrenzen werden weder in Bremen noch in Niedersachsen besonders ernst genommen.

Die Ursprünge Bremens liegen auf einer Düne am Markt. Hier lebten die ersten Bremer. Der Sage nach waren sie Landesflüchtige, die, weserabwärts rudernd, eine neue Heimat suchten und von einer Glucke und ihren Küken auf die Düne gelotst wurden. Wo die sich mit ihrem Nachwuchs sicher fühlt, so sagten sie sich, wollen wir es auch wagen.

Im Jahre 782 trat Bremen mit einem Paukenschlag auf die Bühne der Weltgeschichte. Es war der einzige Paukenschlag, mit dem sich die Bremer in der Weltgeschichte bemerkbar gemacht haben. Paukenschläge passen nicht zum bremischen Wesen.

A village with a tram – that's how the people of Bremen describe their city, with a smile on the face, yet with unconcealed love.

Bremen is truly a city and the capital of the Federal State of Bremen. In the city centre, however, the spires of the Cathedral still tower above the residential properties and business premises – just as they did in the old days.

Bremen is a town of short distances. It takes no time at all to get anywhere. Those in a hurry go by bicycle or, for example, they may take the tram to collect friends from the airport.

To give an idea of the location of the city and the state, we can tell you that Bremen lies at 53° 4′ 15″ North and 8° 48′ 15″ East. One cannot be more precise than that.

The reference point for these coordinates was the spire of St. Ansgar's Church. Although the church no longer exists, the point itself must still be there. Most probably on the well-trodden floor of a shop, in the place where the church once stood. Why not go and look for it?

The lifeline of the state is the River Weser.

The Free Hanseatic City of Bremen lies at the passage from the middle Weser to the lower Weser (at the Weser Weir) and is surrounded by Lower Saxony. However, federal state borders are not taken all that seriously, either by Bremen or by Lower Saxony.

The origins of Bremen go back to a sand dune where the market square is now. This is where the first Bremeners lived. Accord-ing to legend, they were fugitives who, rowing down the Weser, were looking for a new home, and in so doing were lured onto the dune by a mother hen and her chicks. Where she feels secure with her brood, they said to themselves, will surely be worth the risk for us.

In 782 Bremen entered the world stage with a drum beat. It was the only occasion in history when the people of Bremen attracted attention to themselves with a bang. Drum beats do not fit the nature of Bremen folk.

Also, 782 schlossen sich die heidnischen Bremer der sächsischen Revolte gegen die Franken und gegen die christlichen Missionare an. Bei der Gelegenheit schlugen sie den Missionar Gerval und einige seiner Freunde tot – und damit wurde Bremen zum ersten Male genannt.

Genutzt hat die Revolte nichts. Die Franken unter Karl dem Großen siegten. Die christlichen Missionare setzten sich in Bremen fest und bauten auf dem höchsten Punkt der Düne eine Kirche. Heute steht dort der große Bremer Dom.

Wir aber stehen im 21. Jahrhundert – mit Blick auf eben diesen zweitürmigen Dom, mitten in Bremens »guter Stube«.

Links von uns, in seiner ganzen Renaissanceschönheit, erhebt sich das im Kern gotische Rathaus mit dem Roland davor, dem Wahrzeichen Bremens. Beide gehören zum Weltkulturerbe.

Rechts von uns bieten die Kaufleute mit ihrem Haus, dem Schütting, der Stadtregierung die Stirn. Halbrechts, in einem repräsentativen Bau von 1966, sitzt die Bürgerschaft und blickt den Regierenden auf die Finger.

Alle Wege in Bremen führen zum Markt. Dort trifft man einander, weil jeder Bremer, der in der Innenstadt zu tun hat, eigentlich täglich über den Markt geht. Auf dem Markt wird geschnackt. Er ist das Konferenzzimmer der Bremer.

Vom Markt aus führt die Böttcherstraße, das Backsteindenkmal Bremer Pioniergeistes und Mäzenatentums, zur Weser hin. Die Straße ist nur 100 Meter lang, aber man kann sich darin einen ganzen Tag aufhalten.

An der Schlachte, dem jüngst umgestalteten historischen Schiffsanlegeplatz, promenieren die Bremer.

Ein Katzensprung ist es zum Schnoorviertel, wo die ersten Fährleute und Fischer lebten. Später war es das Viertel der Handwerker. Heute sind im Schnoor viele Künstler und Kunsthandwerker zu Hause, dazu gibt es viele Gasthäuser und mehrere Theater.

Der Wall mit Wallgraben umschließt mit seinem Grün das Zentrum Bremens. Auf einer der alten Bastionen erhebt sich eine Windmühle.

So it was that, in 782, the heathen Bremeners joined the Saxon revolt against the Franks and the Christian missionaries. On this occasion they killed the missionary Gerval and some of his followers – and thus, for the first time, Bremen entered the pages of history.

The revolt, however, was to no avail. The Franks under Charlemagne were victorious. The Christian missionaries settled in Bremen and built a church on the highest point of the dune. This is where Bremen's imposing Cathedral stands today.



We, in the 21st century, find ourselves in the middle of the "parlour" of Bremen looking at this twin-spired Cathedral.

On our left, in all its Renaissance splendour, we see the originally Gothic Town Hall and in front of it the statue of Roland, the emblem of Bremen. Both are World Heritage Sites.

To our right, the Schütting, the merchants' Guild Hall, faces the government buildings. Half-right, the city councillors, in their prestigious building dating from 1966, keep a close eye on those who govern.

In Bremen, all roads lead to the market square. Here, people meet one another, because every Bremener who has some business to do in the city centre walks across the market square practically every day. In the market square people stop for a gossip; it is the "conference room" of the people of Bremen.

Leading from the market square towards the Weser is Böttcherstraße, a brick memorial to the pioneering spirit and patronage of Bremen. The street is only 100 metres long, but one could spend a whole day there.

The people of Bremen go for a stroll along the Schlachte, the recently re-designed historic boat moorings.

From there, it's only a stone's throw to the Schnoorviertel, the quarter where the first ferrymen and fishermen used to live. Later on it became the tradesmen's quarter. Today, the Schnoor is home to many artists and craft workers, and there are also numerous restaurants and several theatres.

Durch das Ostertor, heute zusammen mit der Kunsthalle ein Museumszentrum, erreichen wir, vorbei am Theater am Goetheplatz, das Ostertorviertel. Es ist eine wohnliche Vorstadt, ein lebendiges Quartier mit zahlreichen Kulturstätten, In-Kneipen und – das Weser-Stadion ist nicht weit.

Vom Hauptbahnhof aus sind es wenige Minuten bis zum Bürgerpark. Er ist einer der ältesten Volksparks in Deutschland. Die Bremer lieben ihn. Aber sie lieben auch die Parks und Gärten überall in der Stadt. Und mit heimlichem Stolz verweisen sie auf ihre Universität. Nicht zuletzt durch sie gelangte Bremen in den Rang einer »Stadt der Wissenschaft«.



Auf dem linken Weserufer liegt die Neustadt, ein zunehmend attraktiveres Wohnquartier. Sie hat sich mit neuen Stadtvierteln nach Süden hin ausgebreitet.

Die Neustadt ist aber auch mit Kaffee, Bier und Schokolade, mit Flughafen und Raumfahrtzentrum verbunden. Autos werden im Osten Bremens gebaut.

Auch der größe stadtbremische Hafen liegt auf der Neustädter Seite. Das alte Hafenrevier befindet sich auf der Altstadtseite. Einer von ihnen, der traditionsreiche Überseehafen, wurde zugeschüttet – eine für Bremer schmerzhafte Operation. Auf ihm und um ihn herum entsteht die Überseestadt. Das lindert den Schmerz.

Hinter dem prosaischen Namen Bremen-Nord verbergen sich einige der liebenswertesten Stadtviertel Bremens. Zum Beispiel Vegesack. Hier bauten die Bremer um 1620 den ältesten künstlichen Hafen Deutschlands. Vegesack war ein Schiffbauplatz der Bremer, und die Kapitäne wohnten dort – nur wenige Schritte von der Weser entfernt.

Ein Abstecher führt in die Künstlerdörfer Worpswede und Fischerhude. Nun ja, sie liegen in Niedersachsen. Aber ohne Bremen, ohne Bremer Mäzene wären diese bekannten Künstlerkolonien nicht entstanden.

60 Kilometer weserabwärts von Bremen liegt die Stadt Bremerhaven, die zum Land Bremen gehört. Verbunden werden die beiden Schwestern durch Autobahn, Eisenbahn und – eben durch die Weser.

The city walls with their moats and greens surround the centre of Bremen. A windmill rises up on one of the old bastions.

Passing through the Ostertor – which today together with the Kunsthalle forms a museum centre – and continuing along the Theater am Goetheplatz, we reach the Ostertorviertel. It is a residential suburb, a lively area with numerous places of cultural interest and fashionable pubs; and the Weser Stadium isn't far away.

From the main station it takes just a few minutes to get to the Bürgerpark. It is one of the oldest public parks in Germany. The Bremeners love it. But they also love all the other parks and gardens in their city. And with a secret pride they mention their University. After all, it played a major role in Bremen gaining the title of "City of Science".

On the left bank of the Weser is the Neustadt district, a residential area which is becoming ever more attractive. It has spread out to the south creating new districts.

Neustadt is also associated with coffee, beer and chocolate, with the airport and the space centre. In the east of Bremen cars are manufactured.

Bremen's biggest harbour is also located on the Neustadt bank. The old harbour quarters are on the old town side. The historic international harbour has been filled in – a painful experience for the Bremeners. However, on it and around it the international city develops, which is some sort of consolation.

Behind the prosaic name of Bremen-Nord lie some of the most charming districts of Bremen, for example Vegesack. Here, in 1620, the people of Bremen built the first man-made harbour in Germany. Vegesack was the Bremeners' shipyard and the sea captains lived there just a few paces from the Weser.

A short detour leads us to the artists' villages of Worpswede and Fischerhude. In fact, they are located in Lower Saxony. But without Bremen and without Bremen's patrons, these well-known artists' colonies would not be in existence today.

60 kilometres down the Weser from Bremen is the town of Bremerhaven, which belongs to the Federal State of Bremen.

Der Weg über die Autobahn dauert etwa eine halbe Stunde. Mit der Eisenbahn ist man im günstigsten Fall ebenso lange unterwegs. Am schönsten ist aber eine Schiffsreise zwischen den beiden Städten, die etwa vier Stunden dauert.

Die Stadt an der Wesermündung wurde 1827 von den Bremern gegründet. Bremen konnte damals wegen der Versandung der Weser nicht mehr von großen Schiffen angelaufen werden.

Bremerhaven wurde die Hafenstadt Bremens. In Bremerhaven, vor allem an der Stromkaje, werden die großen Containerschiffe abgefertigt. Der Hafen ist bedeutender Autoumschlagplatz, und Bremerhavener Werften halten die Fahne des traditionellen bremischen Schiffbaus hoch.

In Bremerhaven gibt es Fischindustrie, das Alfred-Wegener-Institut für Polar- und Meeresforschung, das Deutsche Schifffahrtsmuseum mit der Kogge von 1380, das Auswandererhaus und den »Zoo am Meer«.

Der Bremerhavener aber liebt seinen Weserdeich, wo der Strom breit und breiter wird. Hier schaut er auf die Nordsee – und auf die Bremer, die sich vor seiner Haustür den Seewind um die Nase wehen lassen wollen.

The two "sisters" are connected by motorway, by railway and, of course, by the Weser.

By motorway the journey takes about half an hour. By rail it takes at least as long – if one is lucky. But the nicest way to go is by taking a boat trip between the two towns which lasts about four hours.

The town at the mouth of the Weser was founded in 1827 by the Bremeners. At that time, Bremen could no longer be accessed by large vessels because of the silting-up of the river.



Bremerhaven became the harbour for Bremen. In Bremerhaven, particularly along the Stromkaje, big container ships are handled. The harbour is a major port of transshipment for cars and Bremerhaven's shipyards continue to fly the flag for Bremen's shipbuilding tradition.

Bremerhaven has a fishing industry, the Alfred Wegener Institute for Polar and Marine Science, the German Maritime Museum with a cog dating from 1380, the Emigrants' House, and the Zoo by the Sea.

The people of Bremerhaven love their Weser dyke where the river becomes ever wider. Here, they can look out to the North Sea – and at the Bremeners who come to breathe the fresh sea air of the big wide world beyond their front door.

Blick vom Schütting: Das gotische Rathaus (1404–1407) mit der von Lüder von Bentheim 1609 bis 1612 gestalteten Renaissancefassade. Davor steht seit 1404 der Roland. Beide überdauerten den Bombenkrieg und gehören seit 2005 zum UNESCO-Weltkulturerbe.

View from the Schütting (Guild Hall): The Gothic Town Hall (1404 – 1407) with Lüder von Bentheim's 1609–1612 Renaissance façade. In front, the statue of Roland which has been there since 1404. Both survived the wartime bombings and in 2005 were designated UNESCO World Heritage Sites.

Staatsbesuch im Rathaus, während die Bremer auf dem Markt die Sonne genießen – oder den Schatten.

State visit at the Town Hall, while the people of Bremen enjoy the sun – or the shade – in the market square.

Herolde bewachen das von zwölf Pfeilern gestützte Rathaus mit seiner steinernen Bilderbuch-Fassade.

Heralds keep watch over the Town Hall with its twelve pillars and its stone picture-book façade.

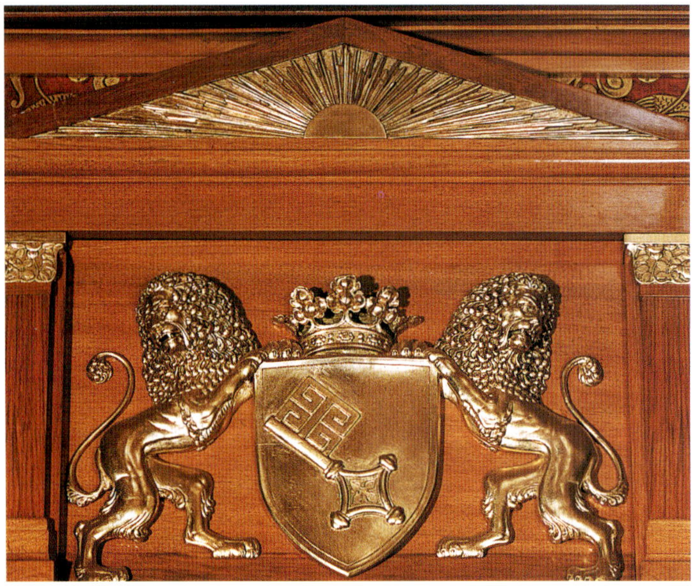

Die Güldenkammer im Alten Rathaus entstand 1609 bis 1612. Ihren Namen erhielt sie 1620 durch ihre gold-rot geprägte Ledertapete. Heinrich Vogeler verwandelte sie 1904 in ein Jugendstil-Juwel.

The Gold Chamber in the old Town Hall dates from 1609 to 1612. It was given its name in 1620 because of the golden-red embossed leather wallpaper. In 1904 Heinrich Vogeler transformed it into an Art-Nouveau gem.

Schaffermahlzeit des Hauses Seefahrt in der Oberen Rathaushalle – das älteste Freundschaftsmahl der Welt.

Schaffermahlzeit, a banquet for sea captains and merchants, held  in the Town Hall's Upper Chamber, is the oldest of its kind in the world and is in support of the Haus Seefahrt Foundation.

Der Bildschmuck der Oberen Halle spiegelt die Geschichte der Stadt seit 782 wider.

The paintings adorning the Upper Chamber illustrate the history of the town since 782.

»Backbord, Steuerbord, Mittschiffs – gode Reis!« Mit Seefahrtsbier aus Silberhumpen wird bei der Schaffermahlzeit angestoßen, dann rauchen die Tonpfeifen.

"Port side, starboard, midships – good journey!" This toast with shipboard beer in silver tankards is given during the Schaffermahlzeit, then clay pipes are smoked.

Silberner Tischschmuck von 1895: Die Pretiosen zieren nur zu besonderen Anlässen wie dem Schaffermahl die Festtafel.

Silver tableware from 1895: these precious items adorn the banquet table only on special occasions, such as the Schaffermahlzeit.

1653r
Rüdeshr

Das köstliche Fundament des Rathauses: der Ratskeller. Hier lagern die ältesten und die besten deutschen Weine, hier winken Trinkgenuss und gutes Essen.

The exquisite foundations of the Town Hall: the Ratskeller. Here the oldest and best German wines are stored and good food and drink can be enjoyed.

Auf dem Marktplatz ist immer etwas los. Die Westseite des Marktplatzes erinnert an alte Bürgerhausarchitektur.

There is always something going on in the market square. The west side of the market square recalls the architecture of former merchants' residences.

Der Roland zu Bremen von 1404 gilt als die größte erhaltene frei stehende Plastik der damaligen Zeit diesseits der Alpen. Der Roland ist ein Symbol für Marktgerechtigkeit, Gerichtsbarkeit und Freiheit. Er ist 5,55 Meter hoch. Die Säule hinter ihm misst vom Sockel bis zur Spitze des Baldachins 10,21 Meter. Bremer, die ihre Stadt für einige Zeit verlassen, melden sich bei ihm ab und streichen über seinen Stein – damit sie gesund zurückkehren.

Roland of Bremen dating from 1404 is thought to be the largest free-standing statue from those times north of the Alps. It symbolises market rights, justice and freedom. The statue is 5.55 m high and the pillar behind measures 10.21 m from the base to the top of the canopy. Bremeners, leaving their town for a while, notify Roland by stroking the stone to guarantee a safe return.

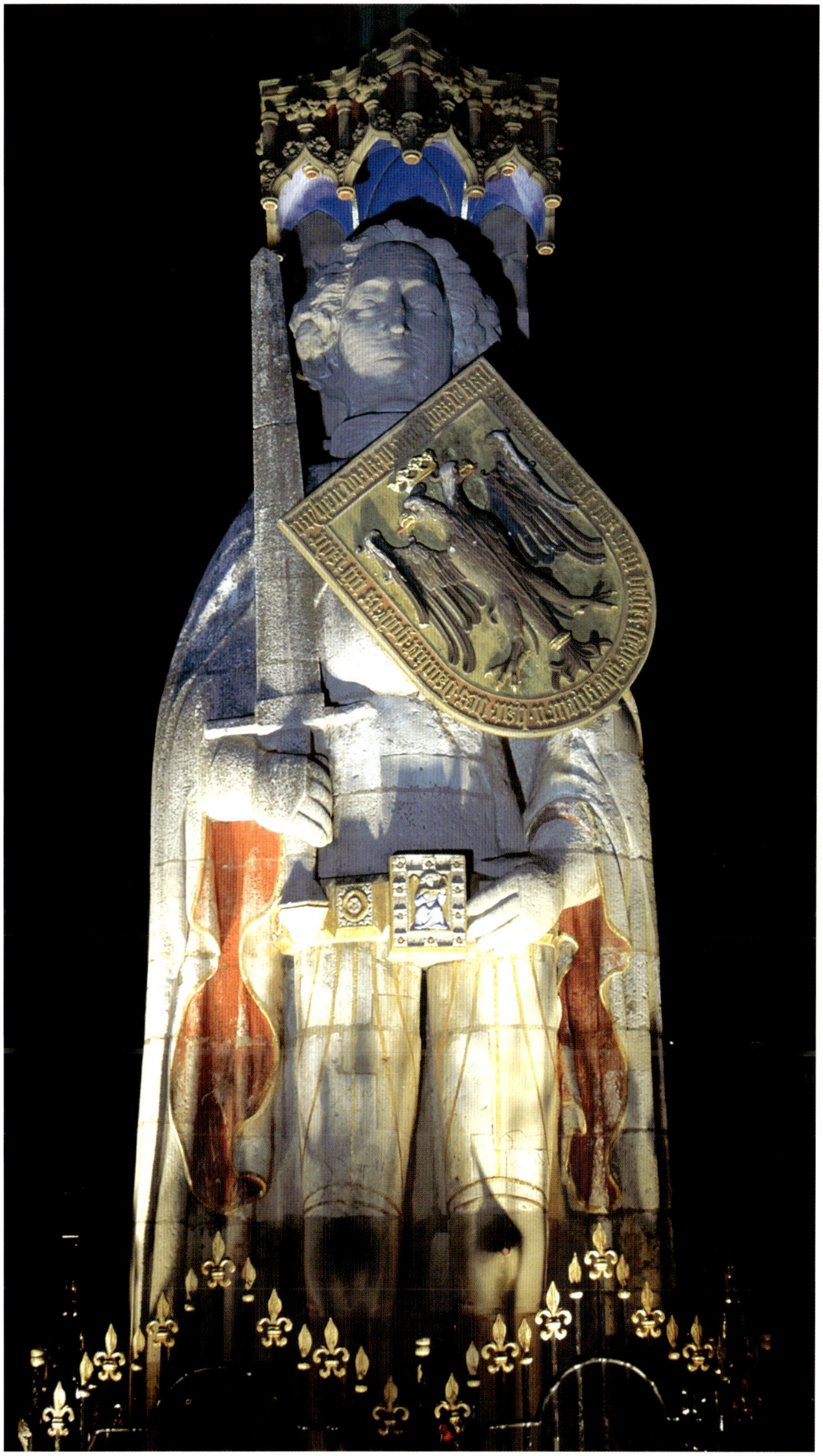

Der Schütting, das Haus der Kaufleute, steht seit 1537/38 am Markt. Der Name stammt wahrscheinlich aus Bergen, wo der »Scoting« ein im Winter Schutz gewährendes Haus der Kaufleute war.

The Schütting, the merchants' Guild Hall, has stood in the market square since 1537/38. The name probably originated in Bergen where the so-called "Scoting" was a building offering shelter to merchants during the winter months.

»Buten un Binnen/Wagen un Winnen« – dieser Satz von Bürgermeister Otto Gildemeister (1823–1902) gilt als Wahlspruch der Bremer Kaufleute und ist über dem Eingang des Schüttings geschrieben.

"Out and in/dare and win" – this motto of Bremen merchants is attributable to Mayor Otto Gildemeister (1823–1902) and is inscribed above the entrance to the Schütting.

Das Haus der Bremischen Bürgerschaft, Sitz des Landesparlaments, steht seit 1966 am Markt. Es entstand nach einem Entwurf des Architekten Wassili Luckhardt.

The Haus der Bürgerschaft in the market square is the Bremen parliament building. It dates from 1966 and was designed by the architect Wassili Luckhardt.

28

Der Bildhauer Gerhard Marcks schuf 1953 die Bremer Stadtmusikanten, die an der Westseite des Rathauses stehen.

The statue to the Town Musicians of Bremen on the west side of the Town Hall was created by the sculptor Gerhard Marcks in 1953.

Zusammen mit dem Roland gleich um die Ecke sind die Stadtmusikanten die meistfotografierten Bremer. Das Märchen von den mutigen Tieren wird in allen Sprachen auf der ganzen Welt erzählt.

Together with Roland, just around the corner, the Town Musicians are the most photographed Bremeners. The fairy tale of the bold animals is told throughout the world in virtually every language.

Buntes Leben im Zentrum: Markttreiben und zwischendurch Seele und Beine baumeln lassen.

Life is colourful in the centre: hustle and bustle in the market square but also a chance to chill out and relax.

Blumenmarkt auf dem Liebfrauenkirchhof – eine für die Innenstadt typische Duftnote.

Flower market in the grounds of the Church of Our Lady – a scene typical of the city centre.

32 Die Liebfrauenkirche, die Kirche des Rates der Stadt, gibt es seit 1000 Jahren.

The Church of Our Lady, the diocesan church, has been in existence for 1000 years.

Sakraler Kunstgenuss seit 1973: Alfred Manessier schuf die Kirchenfenster von Liebfrauen.

The enjoyment of sacred art since 1973: Alfred Manessier created the windows in the Church of Our Lady.

Marktleben mit Höhepunkten: Dazu gehört die Eröffnung der Matjessaison Anfang Juni.

Highlights of market life: these include the beginning of the herring season in early June.

Domshof: Am Neptunbrunnen in der Sonne sitzen oder einen Stock höher kaffeesieren.

Domshof: sitting in the sun by Neptune's fountain or enjoying a coffee one floor up.

Etwas eitel spiegelt sich der Dom in der Glasfassade des Hauses der Bürgerschaft.

Somewhat vainly perhaps the Cathedral mirrors itself in the glass façade of the parliament building.

Der Dom St. Petri gehört zu den wichtigsten Sehenswürdigkeiten der Stadt. Allein schon Ost- und Westkrypta, die zu den ältesten Räumen in Bremen gehören, sind von einzigartiger Schönheit. Nicht vergessen sollte man einen Besuch im Dommuseum und im Bleikeller. Er ist mit seinen Mumien die Gruselkammer der Stadt.

St. Peter's Cathedral is one of the principal highlights of the city. The East and West Crypts, which are amongst the oldest interiors in Bremen, are of exceptional beauty. A visit to the Cathedral Museum and the Lead Cellar is a must. The latter, with its mummies, is the city's horror chamber.

Der Dom in seiner jetzigen Größe geht zurück auf Erzbischof Bezelin (1035–1043).

The Cathedral, as seen today, goes back to the time of Archbishop Bezelin (1035–1043).

Die Zeit läuft, schon ist man 30 Jahre alt und nicht verheiratet: Ein Grund, unter den Blicken der Turmbläser und Bismarcks Klinken zu putzen und zu feiern.

Old customs die hard. Time is passing by, one is already 30 years old and not yet married: good reason to polish door handles under the eyes of horn blowers and Bismarck and to celebrate.

Junggesellen, die 30 Jahre alt werden, müssen die Domtreppen fegen.

While bachelors who reach 30 years of age must sweep the Cathedral steps.

42

Der Bremer Weihnachtsmarkt im Zentrum der Stadt gehört zu den schönsten und beliebtesten in Deutschland.

The Bremen Christmas Market in the city centre is one of the most beautiful and most popular in Germany.

St. Georg kämpft mit dem Drachen und bewacht die Böttcherstraße.

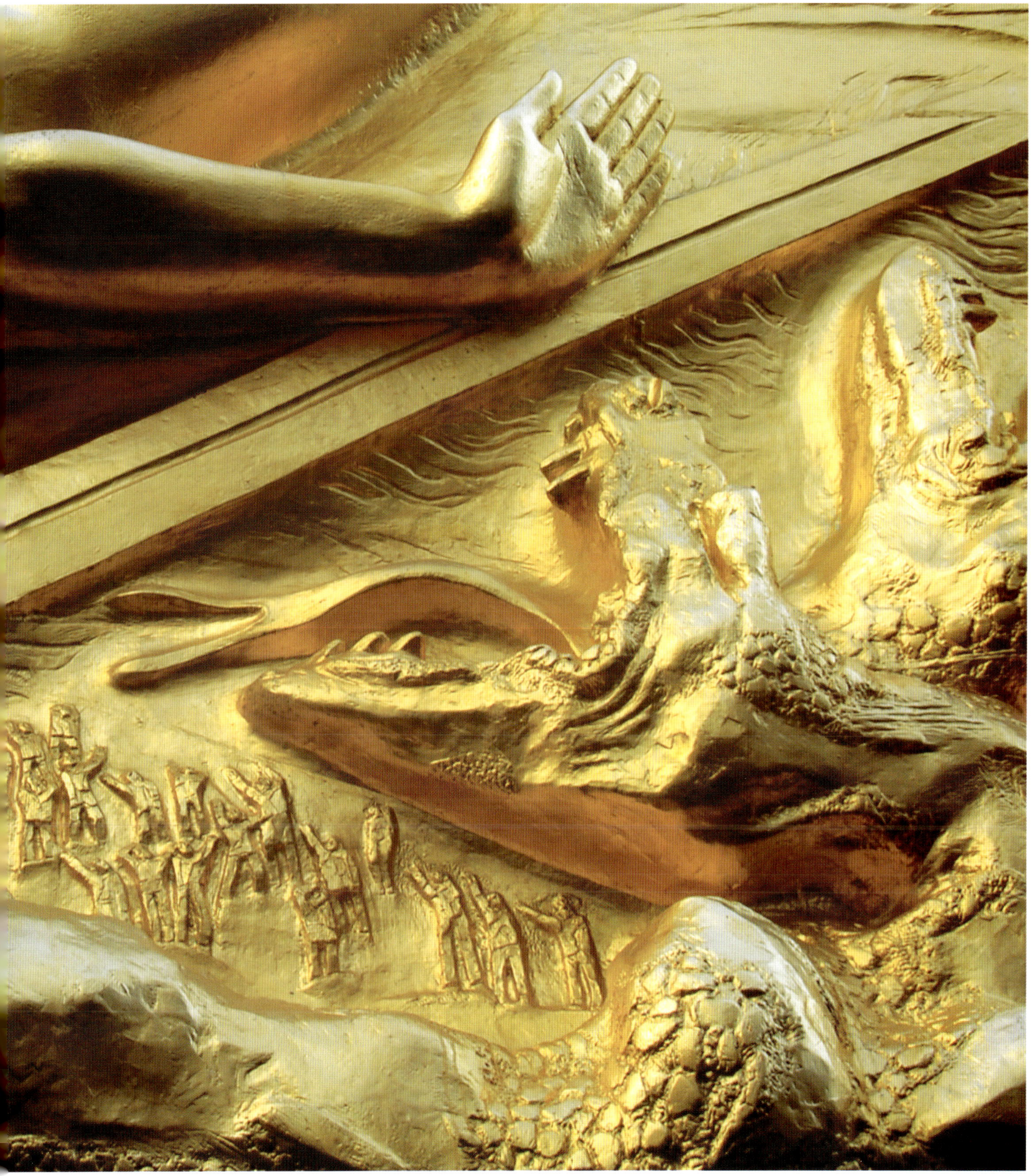

St. George fights the dragon and keeps watch over Böttcherstraße.

Museen, Kunsthandwerk, Gastronomie und eine Spielbank prägen das Bild der Straße.

Museums, handicrafts, gastronomy, and a casino characterise this street.

Die Böttcherstraße wurde von 1924 bis 1931 von den Architekten Runge, Scotland und Hoetger gestaltet.

Böttcherstraße was re-built between 1924 and 1931 based on a design by the architects Runge, Scotland and Hoetger.

Das Glockenspiel in der Böttcherstraße ertönt seit 1934. Die 30 Meißener Porzellanglocken wurden zuletzt 1991 ausgetauscht.

The glockenspiel in Böttcherstraße has been chiming since 1934. The 30 Meißen porcelain bells were last exchanged in 1991.

Der Eingang zum Paula-Becker-Modersohn-Haus in der Böttcherstraße mit der Plastik »Mutter und Kind« von Bernhard Hoetger.

The entrance to the Paula Becker-Modersohn House in Böttcherstraße with its sculpture "Mother and Child" by Bernhard Hoetger.

Drei Figurengruppen von Hoetger: die »Sieben Faulen« und die »Stadtmusikanten« im Handwerkerhof, zwei Panter vor dem Robinson-Crusoe-Haus.

Three sculptures by Hoetger: the "Seven Idlers" and the "Town Musicians" in the Handwerkerhof and two panthers in front of the Robinson Crusoe House.

52 Der Himmelssaal im Haus Atlantis in der Böttcherstraße – ein architektonisches Meisterwerk von Bernhard Hoetger (1874–1949).

The Himmelssaal (Sky Chamber) in the Atlantis House in Böttcherstraße – an architectural masterpiece by Bernhard Hoetger (1874–1949).

SCHNOOR
OASE

Wüstestätte im Schnoorviertel. Aus Platznot in ihren viel zu kleinen Wohnungen feierten noch Mitte des 20. Jahrhunderts die Bewohner ihre Familienfeste unter freiem Himel vor ihren Haustüren. Heute genießen dort Gäste aus aller Welt das historische Ambiente.



Wüstestätte in the Schnoorviertel. As recently as the mid-20th century the residents celebrated family occasions out-of-doors as there was not sufficient room inside their tiny apartments. These days, visitors from all over the world enjoy the historic ambience.

Bunte Palette im Schnoor: Marionetten, Schmuck und eine Erinnerung an die 1981 verstorbene »Mutter Hocke« in ihrem heute noch bestehenden Drehorgelverleih.

Colourful scenes in Schnoor: puppets, jewellery and a reminder of "Mother Hocke", who died in 1981, and her hurdy-gurdy rental shop which exists to this day.

Die Straße Schnoor – »schnur«gerade.

Schnoor – a narrow street like a "piece of string".

Weihnachtsstimmung am Stavendamm, wo früher die beheizten Badestuben standen.

A feeling of Christmas at Stavendamm, where at one time heated bath houses were located.

Im Schutze der Kirche St. Johann entwickelte sich das Schnoorviertel. Historischer und aktueller Fassadenschmuck.

The Schnoorviertel flourished under the protective eye of St. John's Church. Historic and contemporary façade decorations.

Das älteste Stadtquartier bietet heute ein buntes und quirliges Bild.

Today, the oldest town quarter has a colourful and lively atmosphere.

In Bremen gibt es seit 2002 wieder ein Kloster: das Birgittenkloster im Schnoorviertel, nicht weit von St. Johann.

There has been a nunnery again in Bremen since 2002: the Birgitte Nunnery in the Schnoorviertel, not far from St. John's.

Die »Glocke« am Dom, benannt nach dem Aussehen ihres Vorgängerbaus, ist ein beliebter Veranstaltungsort.

The "Glocke" by the Cathedral, named after the bell-like appearance of the previous building on this site, is a popular centre for events.

In den Sälen der »Glocke« finden vor allem Konzerte statt. Restaurant und Garten laden zur Erholung ein.

Mainly concert performances are held in the halls of the "Glocke". A restaurant and a garden are an invitation to relax.

Das Gerichtshaus an der Domsheide, ein wuchtiges, schlossartiges Gebäude, entstand 1891 bis 1895. Zwischen dem Justizgebäude und der Stadtbibliothek lockt ein Biergarten. Der Innenhof wird für Veranstaltungen genutzt und beim Musikfest illuminiert.

The Court House in Domsheide, a huge castle-like structure, was built between 1891 and 1895. An inviting beer garden is to be found between the judicial building and the City Library. The courtyard is used for events and is illuminated during the Music Festival.

Weserrenaissance in der Langenstraße: Kaufmannshaus mit kunstvoll gestalteter Fassade.

Architecture in the so-called Weser Renaissance style in Langenstraße: merchant's house with ornate façade.

Die Stadtwaage, erbaut 1586–88, ist seit 2001 Sitz der Günter-Grass-Stiftung.

Stadtwaage, the former weighing house, dating from 1586–88, has been home to the Günter Grass Foundation since 2001.

1618–21 errichtet, 1944 zerstört und 1952–59 aufwändig wiederhergestellt: das Gewerbehaus auf dem St. Ansgarii-Kirchhof.

Built 1618–1621, destroyed 1944, and then re-built 1952–1959 with no expense spared: the Trade Hall in the grounds of St. Ansgar's Church.

Die Obernstraße. Sie ist eine der Hauptgeschäftsstraßen der Stadt.

Obernstraße: one of the city's main shopping streets.

Zu den Einkaufszentren gehört auch die Sögestraße. Seit den 1970er-Jahren ist sie Fußgängerzone.

Sögestraße is also part of the shopping area. It has been a pedestrian precinct since the 1970s.

Von der Sögestraße aus führen Passagen zu vielen kleinen Geschäften.

Arcades with many small shops lead off Sögestraße.

Mitten in der Stadt steht die Mühle am Wall – eine von insgesamt fünf Mühlen in Bremen.

The Mill on the Wall in the centre of the city – one of five mills in Bremen.

Zwischen Innenstadt und Bahnhofsviertel trifft man am Wall auf mächtige Bäume.

There are many huge trees along the city wall between the city centre and the station.

Die alten Bastionen mit dem Stadtgraben wurden ab 1802 zu einer Parklandschaft, in der sich bedeutende Kunstwerke befinden. Einige werden, etwa zum Wallfest im Juli, illuminiert. Linke Seite rechts unten: der Astronom und Arzt Wilhelm Olbers (1758–1840).

The old city fortifications have been developed as parklands from 1802 onwards and many important works of art are to be found here. During the Wall Festival in July some are illuminated. Opposite page, bottom right: the astronomer and doctor Wilhelm Olbers (1758–1840).

Doppelte Begegnung mit Claude Monets »Camille« in der Bremer Kunsthalle.

Double encounter with Claude Monet's "Camille" in the Bremen Art Gallery.

Die Kunsthalle am Wall ist bei Kunstliebhabern in aller Welt bekannt.

The Art Gallery by the wall is known to art lovers throughout the world.

THEATER AM GOETHEPLATZ

Kulturzentrum am Ostertor: Das Gerhard Marcks-Haus und die Wilhelm-Wagenfeld-Stiftung befinden sich in den beiden Wachhäusern. Ihnen schließt sich das Theater am Goetheplatz an (links).

Cultural centre at the Ostertor: the Gerhard Marcks House and the Wilhelm Wagenfeld Foundation are housed in the two watch towers. And adjacent to it is the Theater am Goetheplatz (left).

Größter europäischer Samba-Karneval in Bremen: Die sprichwörtlich sturen Bremer und ihre Gäste können sehr ausgelassen feiern.

Europe's biggest samba carnival in Bremen: the proverbially stolid Bremeners and their guests can celebrate boisterously.

La Strada – ein überregional bekanntes und beliebtes »Straßenzirkusfestival« vereinigt Alt und Jung.

La Strada – a widely-known and popular "Street Circus Festival" unites young and old.

Ein Prosit auf die Späße am Rande: La Strada zieht viele gute Künstler an.

A toast to fun at the fringes: La Strada attracts many first-rate artists.

Wenn das Ostertorviertel feiert, ist Gedränge garantiert.

Crowds are guaranteed when the Ostertorviertel celebrates.

Im »Viertel«, wie die Bremer das Ostertor- und Steintorviertel nennen, wohnt und lebt man gemütlich.

In the "Viertel", as the Bremeners call the quarters around the Ostertor and Steintor, people live in pleasant surroundings.

Der Ostertorsteinweg, seit 1359 eine mit Steinen gepflasterte Straße, die Richtung Hamburg führte, ist die Hauptverkehrsader des Quartiers.

Ostertorsteinweg, a cobbled street ever since 1359, which led towards Hamburg, is the district's main artery.

Ein erhaltener Kaufmannsladen aus dem Jahre 1907, Gaststätten aller Art und Musikinstrumentenbauer – alles in enger und freundschaftlicher Nachbarschaft.

A grocery shop dating from 1907, all kinds of restaurants, as well as musical instrument makers – friendly neighbours all bunched together.

Fahrende Tanzflächen mit 350 PS: Wenn sich die »Visionparade« anmeldet, verwandeln Zehntausende den Osterdeich in eine Partymeile.

Moving dance floors at 350hp: when the "Vision Parade" is in sight, tens of thousands of party-goers turn the Osterdeich into a mile of fun.

Die Weser – Lebensader der Freien Hansestadt Bremen.

The River Weser – lifeline of the Free Hanseatic City of Bremen.

Eiswette von 1829: Volksfest und Festessen mit Persönlichkeiten aus Wirtschaft und Politik.

Eiswette (Ice Wager) dating from 1829: folk festival and banquet with business leaders and politicians.

Die »Drei Weisen aus dem Morgenlande« und der »Schneider« spielen bei der Eiswette ihre Rollen.

The "Three Wise Men" and the "Tailor" play their parts during the Eiswette.

Junge Bremer, die auf sich halten, schließen sich einem Ruderverein an.

Young Bremeners with an image to maintain join a rowing club.

Sport, Spaß und Seenotrettung auf der Weser.

Sport, fun and sea rescue on the Weser.

Wasserturm an der Weser, die »umgekippte Kommode« wird manchmal illuminiert.

Water tower on the Weser: the "overturned chest of drawers" is sometimes illuminated.

Segelpartie vor geruhsam kaffeesierenden Bremern und ihren Gästen.

Sailing boat passing Bremeners enjoying coffee with their guests.

Breminale – ein Kulturfest an der Weser.

Breminale – a cultural festival on the Weser.

Die Weser verbindet die Menschen.

The Weser draws people together.

In der Pauliner Marsch, unmittelbar an der Weser gelegen, treffen sich die Familien.

Families get together at the Pauliner Marsch, located on the banks of the Weser.

Von der Gaststätte Jürgenshof sind es nur wenige Schritte zu vielen Sportplätzen.

There are many sports fields only a short distance from the Jürgenshof Restaurant.

Die Stadt ist sportbegeistert – nicht nur wegen Werder Bremen.

The city is passionate about sport – not just because of Werder Bremen.

Allerdings ist die Fußballmannschaft das Aushängeschild – wenn der Club Deutscher Fußballmeister wird, kann vor dem Rathaus kein Apfel zur Erde fallen.

However, it is best known for its football team. When the Club becomes German Football League champion there isn't space for an apple to fall to the ground in front of the Town Hall.

Für die Bremer und ihre Gäste ist die Schlachte ein beliebter Treffpunkt – sie ist Hafenplatz seit 1000 Jahren.

The Schlachte is a popular meeting place for Bremeners and their visitors – it has been a harbour for nearly 1000 years.

Wo noch im 19. Jahrhundert hart gearbeitet wurde, wird heute der Feierabend genossen.

Whereas during the 19th century people worked hard here, today it's a place for relaxation.

Ob Floh- oder Kajenmarkt – an der Weser, fünf Minuten vom Zentrum entfernt, »spielt die Musik«.

Whether a flea market or a market along the quays – by the Weser, five minutes from the centre, "sings a happening".

HANSEAT

Blick von der Neustadtseite über die Innenstadt.

A view from the Neustadt side across the city centre.

Gegenüber der Schlachte liegt die Weserburg mit einem Museum für neuzeitliche Kunst. Die Objekte stammen vorwiegend aus Privatsammlungen.

Opposite the Schlachte is the Weserburg with a museum of contemporary art. The exhibits are mainly from private collections.

Frühmorgendliche Stimmung am Weserstrom.

Early morning scene by the River Weser.

Auf der linken Weserseite entstand im 17. Jahrhundert die Neustadt mit ihren typischen Bremer Häusern.

Neustadt on the left bank of the Weser, with its typical Bremen houses, was first settled in the 17th century.

Centaurenbrunnen und der »kleine« Roland sind die Paten der Neustadt.

The Centaur Fountain and "little" Roland take good care of Neustadt.

Zu den attraktiven Kulturstätten gehört die Shakespeare-Company in der Neustadt.

The Shakespeare Company is one of the popular cultural attractions in Neustadt.

Innerhalb weniger Jahrzehnte hat sich der Airport Bremen zu einem regionalen Drehkreuz gemausert.

Within a few decades Bremen Airport has expanded into a regional hub.

Bremen hat lange Tradition als Stadt des Flugzeugbaus und der Raumfahrt.

Bremen has a long tradition of aeroplane construction and space travel.

Abendstimmung am Werdersee. Das innenstadtnahe Erholungsgebiet entstand, als das vormalige Feucht- und Überschwemmungsgelände 1960 abgedämmt und geflutet wurde.

Evening scene by the Werdersee. This leisure area, close to the city centre, was established in 1960 when a dam was constructed and former wet lands were flooded.

Die Mittelweser, wo sich der Hemelinger Hafen befindet, endet am Weserwehr. Und wo immer es möglich ist, haben sich am Weserufer Kleingärtner niedergelassen.

The middle Weser ends at the Weser Weir where the Hemeling Harbour is located. And wherever possible allotments have been established along the bank.

WERDER
BREMEN

Bremen ist zusammen mit Bremerhaven zweitgrößter Hafenstandort Deutschlands.

Bremen together with Bremerhaven form Germany's second-largest harbour.

Auf stadtbremischem Gebiet wird vor allem der Neustädter Hafen von großen Schiffen angelaufen.

Large vessels dock within the city itself, mainly at the Neustädter Hafen.

Die bremische Nahrungsmittelindustrie hat einen weltweit guten Ruf: Beck's-Bier, Kellogg's, Schokolade von Hachez und viele Marken von Kraft Foods.

Bremen's food industry is of worldwide repute: Beck's beer, Kelloggs products, Hachez chocolates and many brands of Kraft Foods.

Das Hochhaus von Kraft steht für den guten Bremer Kaffee: Jacobs und HAG. Es gibt aber auch noch einige kleine Röster.

The Kraft high-rise building stands for good Bremen coffee: Jacobs and HAG. There are also some smaller roast houses still in existence.

138

Von der Neustadtseite blickt man auf die Steffensstadt mit der Stephani-Kirche. Einst war es das Fischerviertel.

From the Neustadt side one looks across to the Steffensstadt district with St. Stephen's Church. It was once the fishermen's quarter.

Die Faulenstraße, an deren Anfang die Sparkasse am Brill liegt, war und wird wieder ein Zentrum der Stadt sein. Sie ist eine »Parallelstraße« zur Weser.

Faulenstraße, at the start of which is the Sparkasse am Brill, was at one time, and is again becoming, a focal point of the city. It runs parallel to the Weser.

Die »Waller Welle« – Blumenschmuck entlang der Nordstraße im Stadtteil Walle – wurde erstmals 1976 von dem Künstler Gary Rieveschl angepflanzt.

The "Waller Welle" – wavelike flower decorations along Nordstraße in the Walle district – was first planted in 1976 by the artist Gary Rieveschl.

Noch ein bisschen Hafenviertel – doch neue Mieter haben sich bereits etabliert.

Still something of a harbour feeling – but new tenants are already well established.

In den alten Speicher XI am zugeschütteten Überseehafen ist neues Leben eingezogen: z.B. die Hochschule für Künste und das Hafenmuseum.

New life has appeared in the old Warehouse XI by the now in-filled international harbour: for instance, the Art School and the Harbour Museum.

Die stadtbremischen Häfen haben noch heute ihre Funktion, und sei es der zugeschüttete Überseehafen, auf dem sich heute der Großmarkt befindet und die Überseestadt heranwächst.

The city's harbours have a function to this day. Even the in-filled international harbour, where now there is a wholesale market and a growing international city.

Tabak, Kaffee und Baumwolle sind nach wie vor bedeutende Importgüter.

Tobacco, coffee and cotton continue to be major imported goods.

Technik verdrängt die Hafenromantik – und doch bleibt immer noch hier und da ein Platz für kleine Tiere.

Technology is replacing the harbour idyll – and yet, here and there, room is still found for small residents.

Gröpelingen war früher das Wohnquartier der Werftarbeiter. Auf der »AG Weser« wurden Schiffe gebaut – keine Raketen. Eine Rakete erinnert an ein »Luftschloss«, das den Namen Space-Park trägt.

In former times Gröpelingen was where the shipyard workers lived. In the "AG Weser" yards ships were built – not rockets. The rocket is a reminder of the brief tenure of the "castle in the air" called Space Park.

Die Menschen in Gröpelingen leben in kleinen Bremer Häusern und genießen die Freuden des Lebens. Von den Werftarbeitern blieb nur ein Denkmal.

The people of Gröpelingen live in Bremen's small houses and enjoy the pleasures of life. Today, a monument is all that remains of the former shipyard workers.

Die Fatih-Moschee in Gröpelingen wurde 1999 eingeweiht. Ihr Kuppelraum ist mit 5 500 farbigen Kacheln verziert. Die Gemeinde besteht seit 1974.

The Fatih Mosque in Gröpelingen was consecrated in 1999. Its vaulted interior is decorated with 5,500 coloured tiles. The religious community has existed since 1974.

Wer es sucht, findet sein Plätzchen mit Hafenidylle.

Wherever you look you'll find an idyllic spot by the harbour.

Modernes Kontorhaus der Spedition Lexzau, Scharbau GmbH auf einem ausgedienten U-Boot-Bunker. Darunter, in guter Nachbarschaft: Fassfabrikation und Kunst.

Modern premises of the shippers Lexzau, Scharbau GmbH built over a former U-boat bunker. Above, friendly neighbours: barrel makers and artists.

HAUPTBAHN

Der Hauptbahnhof wurde 1886–89 gebaut und hat sich äußerlich kaum verändert (links).
Sport auf dem Bahnhofsvorplatz. Nicht weit davon entfernt: Kunst am Bau (oben).

The main station was built between 1886 and 1889 and has since changed little in outward appearance (left).
Sport on the station concourse. Not far away: "Kunst am Bau", art as part of the building (above).

Die Welt unter dem Dach des Übersee-museum. Bremer Kaufleute legten mit »Souvenirs« den Grundstein für dieses Museum.

The whole world under the roof of the Überseemuseum. Bremen merchants laid a foundation stone of "souvenirs" for this museum.

Den Bremer Freimarkt gibt es seit 1035. Er wird jedes Jahr im Oktober auf der Bürgerweide und in der ganzen Innenstadt als fünfte Jahreszeit gefeiert.

The Bremen Freimarkt has been in existence since 1035. It is celebrated every year in October on the Bürgerweide and throughout the city centre as the Fifth Season.

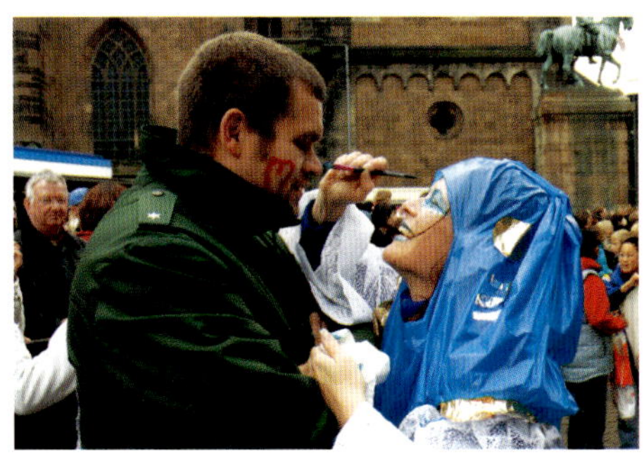

Selbst Roland am Markt feiert den Freimarkt mit.

Even Roland in the market square takes part in the Freimarkt festivities.

Für die Bremer ist ein Besuch des Freimarkts Ehrensache.

For Bremeners, a visit to the Freimarkt is a must.

Die Stadthalle, heute AWD Dome, bietet Raum für viele Großereignisse. Zum Beispiel: Sechs-Tage-Rennen, Musikschau der Nationen, Reitturniere und Holiday on Ice.

The Stadthalle, today called the AWD Dome, accommodates a variety of large events. For instance: six-day bicycle racing, the "Musikschau der Nationen", horse shows and Holiday on Ice.

Im Findorff-Viertel mit dem Kulturzentrum Schlachthof und seinem weithin bekannten Wochenmarkt war früher Endstation der Torfkähne, die Torf aus dem Moor in die Stadt brachten. Heute befördern die Kähne gut gelaunte Passagiere.

In former times, the terminus for peat boats bringing turf from the moor into the city was located in the Findorff district, now famous for its weekly market and the Schlachthof Cultural Centre. Today, historic turf boats carry cheerful passengers.

Der Elefant an der Bürgerweide wurde 1931 als Kolonial-Ehrenmal aufgestellt. Er sollte an die deutschen Kolonien erinnern. Heute steht er als Mahnmal gegen den Kolonialismus.

The elephant on the Bürgerweide was erected in 1931 in commemoration of the German colonies. Today it is a memorial against colonialism.

In Schwachhausen werden die Besucher von einem Kaiser begrüßt: Kaiser Friedrich III. (1831–1888), dem »99-Tage-Kaiser«. Das Denkmal, im Stil römischer Kaiserstatuen errichtet, wurde 1905 enthüllt.

Visitors to Schwachhausen are greeted by an emperor: Frederick III (1831–1888), the "99-Day Emperor". The monument, in the style of the statues of Roman emperors, was unveiled in 1905.

Das typische Bremer Haus im vorderen Schwachhausen.

Typical Bremen houses in Schwachhausen.

Die Bremer schmücken ihre Häuser gern mit kleinen Kunstwerken.

The people of Bremen like to decorate their houses with small artworks.

Seit 1865: Der Bürgerpark, von den Bürgern der Stadt finanziert, ist einer der ältesten deutschen Volksparks.

Since 1865: The Bürgerpark, financed by the citizens of Bremen, is one of the oldest public parks in Germany.

Bordkapelle auf dem Emmasee im Bürgerpark. Darüber: Blick aus der Meierei. Rechts: Biergarten für alle Generationen.

A floating band on the Emmasee in the Bürgerpark. Top: a view from the Meierei Restaurant. Right: beer garden for young and old.

HAAKE-BECK
HAAKE-BECK
HAAKE-BECK
HAAKE-BEC

Der Bürgerpark bietet für jeden Geschmack etwas.

The Bürgerpark offers something for everyone.

Einkehrmöglichkeiten im Bürgerpark: Park Hotel, Meierei, Kaffeehaus am Emmasee – und eine Hängematte.

Places to drop into in the Bürgerpark: Park Hotel, Meierei Restaurant, Kaffeehaus am Emmasee – and a hammock.

Winterstimmung im Bürgerpark mit dem Park Hotel – im Hintergrund die Stadtsilhouette.

Winter scene in the Bürgerpark with the Park Hotel – silhouette of the city in the background.

Bremer Kunst und Kultur gibt es im Focke-Museum zu sehen – und lohnende Sonderausstellungen wie hier »Die letzten Stunden von Herculaneum«.

Bremen art and culture can be seen in the Focke Museum, together with rewarding special exhibitions such as "The Last Hours of Herculaneum" as seen above.

Schon im Mittelalter stand hier ein Gutshaus – heute ist das »Haus Riensberg« Teil des Focke-Museums.

As far back as the Middle Ages there was a manor house here – today "Haus Riensberg" is a part of the Focke Museum.

Der Rhododendronpark in Horn ist vor allem während der Blütezeit ein Anziehungspunkt.

The Rhododendron Park in Horn is a particular attraction when the rhododendrons are in blossom.

Rhododendronpark mit Botanischem Garten, »Botanika« und dem größten liegenden Buddha Europas.

The Rhododendron Park with the Botanic Gardens, "Botanika" and Europe's largest reclining Buddha.

In Schwachhausen, Horn und Oberneuland sind viele herrschaftliche Villen zu entdecken.

Many splendid villas are to be found in Schwachhausen, Horn and Oberneuland.

Der Riensberger Friedhof – viele Prominente fanden dort ihre letzte Ruhe.

The cemetery at Riensberg – many well-known people were laid to rest here.

Dörfliche Idylle in der Großstadt: Mühlenromantik, herrliche Parks und der Golfplatz zwischen Horn und der Neuen Vahr.

Village idyll in the city. Old romantic mills, splendid parks and the golf course between Horn and Neue Vahr.

Fachwerk, Strohdach und Pferdeköpfe auf dem First – Oberneulander Idylle.

Timber frame, thatched roof and horse heads on the ridge – an Oberneuland idyll.

Oldtimer in einer alten Allee, die zu einem Landsitz führt.

Old-timer in an old avenue leading to a country manor house.

Im morgendlichen Dunst: Radfahrer vor der Oberneulander Mühle.

In the early morning haze: a cyclist in front of the Oberneuland Mill.

Ein guter Fensterplatz ist etwas wert.

A good outlook is cherished.

Oberneuland gilt als Pferdeparadies.

Oberneuland is known as a horses' paradise.

Auf dem Wümmedeich: Zweirädrige Oldtimer – um sie zu fahren braucht, man Geschick.

On the Wümme dyke: penny-farthings, two-wheeled old-timers, require skilled riders.

Landleben am Rande der Stadt.

Country living at the edge of town.

18-Loch-Platz in Oberneuland: Golf – nach englischem Vorbild in Bremen ein Volkssport.

18-hole golf course in Oberneuland: golf, modelled on the English style, is a popular sport in Bremen.

Zwischen Universität und Stadtwald wird im »Universum« die Welt der Naturwissenschaften erklärt.

In the "Universum", between the university and the Stadtwald, the world of science is explained.

Ein Tag reicht nicht, um sich das ganze »Universum« zu erschließen. Die Mitmachausstellung wurde 1996 eröffnet.

One day is not sufficient to explore the entire "Universum". The hands-on exhibition was opened in 1996.

Eine Stadt am Stadtrand: die Universität Bremen.

A city on the edge of the city: the University of Bremen.

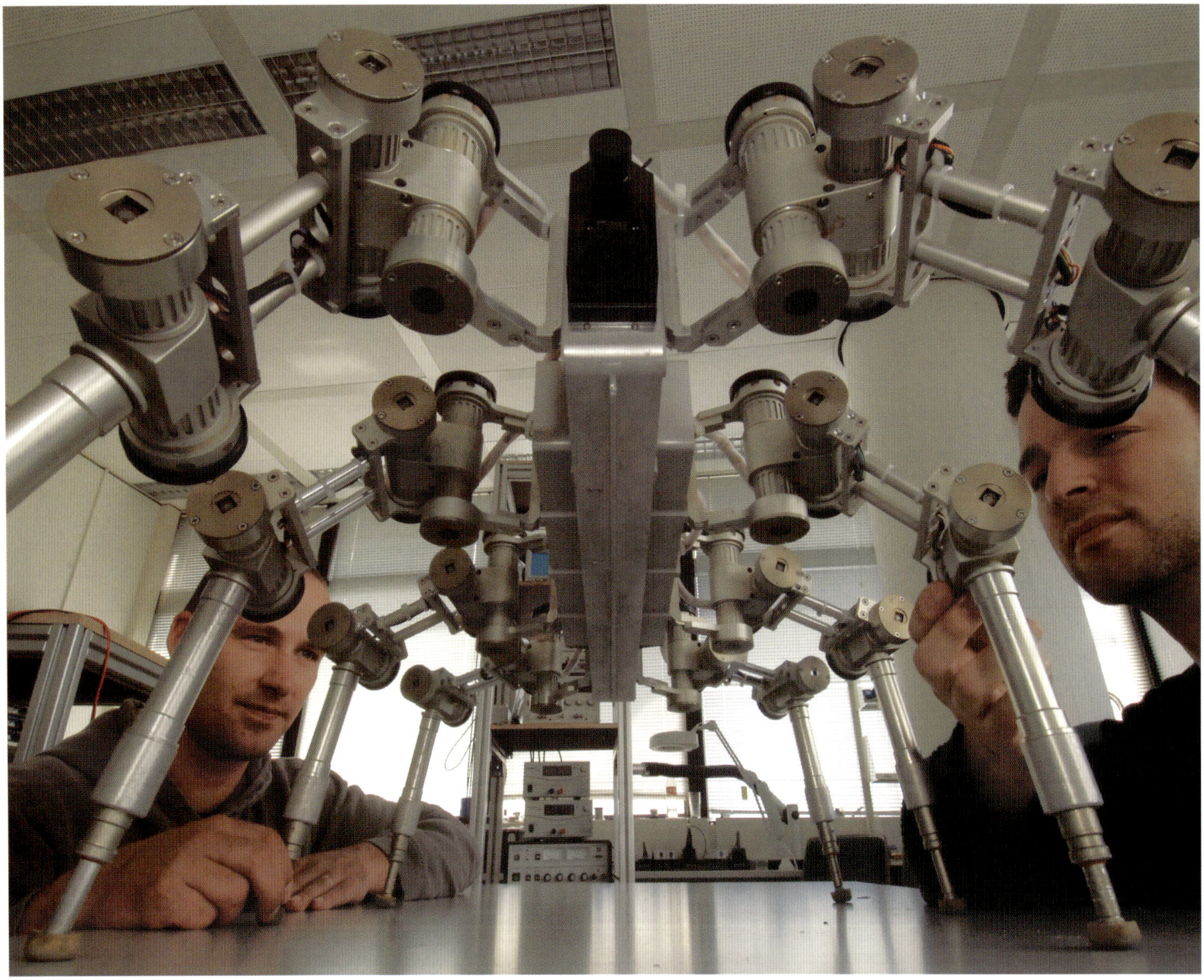

Forschung und Lehre – durch die Universität wurde Bremen zur Stadt der Wissenschaft.

Research and teaching – the university was the driving force in Bremen being named the City of Science.

Im 146 Meter hohen Fallturm wird in Kapseln beim freien Fall Schwerelosigkeit simuliert.

In the 146 m high Drop Tower weightlessness is simulated in a free-fall capsule.

Die Trabrennbahn in der Vahr wurde 1907 angelegt. Eine Bremische Besonderheit: Mittendrin ein Golfplatz.

The trotting course in the Vahr district was laid out in 1907. A Bremen speciality: a golf course in the middle of it.

212 Das 65 Meter hohe Aalto-Hochhaus in der Vahr wurde von dem Finnen Alvar Aalto (1898–1976) entworfen. 1963 zogen die ersten Mieter in Bremens schönstes Wohnhochhaus.

The 65 m high Aalto Hochhaus in Vahr was designed by the Finn Alvar Aalto (1898–1976). The first tenants moved into Bremen's finest apartment block in 1963.

Die Neue Vahr war nach dem Krieg das Vorzeigeviertel der Bremer.

Neue Vahr was the post-war showpiece district of Bremen.

In Bremen-Sebaldsbrück werden bei Daimler-Chrysler verschiedene Mercedes-Modelle gebaut, Silberwaren kommen wie vor 150 Jahren noch immer aus dem Nachbarstadtteil Hemelingen.

Various Mercedes models are manufactured at the Daimler-Chrysler factory in Bremen-Sebaldsbrück. Silverware is still made in the neighbouring district of Hemelingen as it was 150 years ago.

Aus einem Vorwerk in Osterholz-Tenever, das Jahrhunderte im Besitz der Familie von Büren war, entstand die Egestorff-Stiftung.

The Egestorff Foundation was established in the outlying estate of Osterholz-Tenever which, for centuries, had been in the hands of the von Büren family.

Johann Heinrich Egestorff, der letzte private Besitzer des Gutes, vermachte es 1905 einer Stiftung »für würdige alte Männer und Frauen«.

Johann Heinrich Egestorff, the last private owner of the manor house, willed it in 1905 to a foundation in support of "deserving elderly men and women".

218

In Bremen drehen sich noch viele Windmühlenflügel, wie hier im verschneiten Arbergen.

In Bremen many windmill sails are still turning as seen here in snow-covered Arbergen.

Die Stahlwerke Bremen liegen unmittelbar an der Weser im Stadtteil Mittelsbühren.

The Bremen Steel Works are located on the banks of the Weser in the "Mittelbühren" district.

Für unsere Zeit nicht unbedingt typisch: Begegnung von Segelschiffen auf der Weser bei Vegesack.



Not necessarily typical of our times: sailing ships passing on the Weser at Vegesack.

Abschlussfeier in der 1999 gegründeten International University in Bremen-Grohn. Es ist eine private Universität.

Graduation day at the International University in Bremen-Grohn, founded in 1999. It is a private university.

Mit der Lesum, einem Nebenfluss der Weser, beginnt Bremen-Nord mit liebenswerten Ortsteilen und Sehenswürdigkeiten, zu denen auch das Schloss Schönebeck gehört.

Bremen-Nord, with its charming districts and sights, one of which is Schönebeck Castle, begins at the Lesum, a tributary of the Weser.

Albatros

Sommer in Lesmona – ein jährlich wiederkehrendes fröhliches Kulturfest unter freiem Himmel mit prall gefüllten Picknick-Körben.

Sommer in Lesmona – an enjoyable annual cultural festival held in the open with picnic baskets filled to the brim.

Die »Schulschiff Deutschland« in Vegesack steht im reizvollen Gegensatz zu den auf der gegenüberliegenden Weserseite gebauten Luxusyachten.

The sail training ship "Schulschiff Deutschland" in Vegesack – a charming contrast to the modern luxury yachts built on the opposite bank of the Weser.

In Vegesack, einem alten Walfängerort, wurde 1620 der erste künstliche Hafen in Deutschland gebaut.

The first man-made harbour in Germany was built in 1620 in Vegesack, an old whaling station.

Ein Sommertag an und auf der Wümme. Gegenüber liegt Niedersachsen und der Gasthof »Zur Schleuse«, zu dem man sich und sein Fahrrad übersetzen lassen kann.

A summer's day both by and on the Wümme. A ferry takes you and your bicycle to the Zur Schleuse Restaurant on the opposite bank in Lower Saxony.

Kaffeegartenatmosphäre an der Wümme. Rechts und links des Flusses präsentiert sich eine reizvolle Landschaft.

A coffee garden scene by the Wümme. A charming landscape lies to the right and the left of the river.

Zu einer Kohl-und-Pinkel-Fahrt gehört eine Wanderung, bei der man sich vergnügt auf die kulinarischen Freuden in einem Gasthaus vorbereitet.

Participants in a "Kohl-und-Pinkel-Fahrt", a walk in preparation for the traditional culinary delights to follow in a restaurant.

Eislauf im Blockland. Schlittschuhlaufen ist ein traditioneller Volkssport der Bremer.

Ice-skating in the Blockland. It is a traditional sport for all Bremeners.

Der Barkenhoff von Heinrich Vogeler in Worpswede ist heute ein Kulturzentrum.

Heinrich Vogeler's Barkenhoff estate in Worpswede is today a cultural centre.

Worpswede – Künstlerkolonie seit über 100 Jahren.

Worpswede – an artists' colony for over 100 years.

Das Grabmahl der 1907 früh verstorbenen Malerin Paula Modersohn-Becker.

The tomb of the artist Paula Modersohn-Becker who died in 1907 at a young age.

Der Niedersachsen-Stein von Bernhard Hoetger am Weiherberg in Worpswede.

The Niedersachen-Stein by Bernhard Hoetger at the Weiherberg in Worpswede.

Die Kunst ist überall im Künstlerdorf Worpswede greifbar.

Art is all-pervasive in the artists' colony of Worpswede.

248 Ohne seine reizvolle Umgebung wäre Worpswede kein Künstlerdorf geworden.

But for its charming surroundings Worpswede would not have become an artists' colony.

Frühmorgendliche Stimmung mit Torfkähnen auf der Hamme.

Early morning scene on the Hamme with turf boats.

Ausflugsziel der Bremer: Fischerhude mit seinen bäuerlichen Gaststätten, in denen regionale Kost auf den Tisch gebracht wird.

A destination for an outing by Bremeners: Fischerhude with its rustic restaurants where regional fare is served.

Fischerhude ist ein Dorf geblieben – mit Landwirten, Künstlern und Galeristen. Am Rande des Dorfes: das Otto-Modersohn-Museum.

Fischerhude has remained a village – with farmers, artists and gallery owners. At the edge of the village: the Otto Modersohn Museum.

Einer der vielen Wümmearme in Fischerhude.

One of the many arms of the Wümme in Fischerhude.

Wenn historische Großsegler zu Gast sind, bietet die Seestadt viele schöne Aussichtspunkte. Die 1921 in Kiel gebaute Viermastbark »Sedov« passiert das alte Ostfeuer – den Pingelturm – an der Kaiserschleuse.

Historic sailing ships visiting the port are an attractive sight. The four-masted barque "Sedov", built in Kiel in 1921, passes the old east lighthouse – the "Pingelturm" – at the Kaiserschleuse (Emperor's Sluice).

Wenn sich in Bremerhaven Segelschiffe aus aller Welt treffen, ist das ein Magnet für Gäste aus ganz Deutschland.

When sailing ships from across the world meet in Bremerhaven it is a magnet for visitors from all over Germany.

Die so oft tot gesagte Hafenromantik lebt in Bremerhaven wieder auf.

New life is breathed into the otherwise bygone romantic harbour atmosphere in Bremerhaven.

Wo sich das Land Bremen als maritime Sehenswürdigkeit präsentiert – in Bremerhaven hinter dem Weserdeich. Dazu gehört das Deutsche Schiffahrtsmuseum mit dem Museumshafen

Maritime sights in the state of Bremen - behind the Weser dyke in Bremerhaven. These include the German Maritime Museum with the Harbour Museum.

Und auch das gehört dazu: Nebel. Der Feind der Seeleute hat durch moderne Technik viel von seinem Schrecken verloren.

And this is part of it too: fog. With the advent of modern technology this enemy of the sailor has now lost much of its terror.

Bremerhaven hat für das Auge viel zu bieten: den Zoo am Meer und die »Bürger«, Hauptstraße der Stadt, Leuchttürme, die Weser und große Kreuzfahrt- und Container-Schiffe.

In Bremerhaven there is much to behold: the Zoo by the Sea and the "Bürger", the main street of the town, lighthouses, the Weser, and large cruise liners and container ships.

Bremerhaven war einer der großen Auswandererhäfen – Auswandererhaus und Schiffahrtsmuseum geben Auskunft.

Bremerhaven was one of the great emigration ports – this is documented in the Emigrants' House and the Maritime Museum.

In Bremerhaven an der Weser befindet sich der größte Autoumschlagsplatz Europas.

Bremerhaven on the Weser has one of the biggest car transshipment facilities in Europe.

Der Containerterminal in Bremerhaven boomt. Die mächtigen Carrier bestimmen das Bild.

The Bremerhaven container terminal is booming. Huge carriers dominate the scene.

Die Containerschiffe werden immer größer, brauchen immer mehr Umschlagfläche, und der Bremer Hafenbau stellt sich darauf ein.

The container ships are getting ever bigger and ever more space is required for transshipment. Bremen's port facilities do justice to this need.

In Bremerhaven wird die Tradition des Schiffbaus fortgeführt, und nach wie vor kann man im Kaiserhafen ein letztes Bier vor der Reise nach New York trinken.

In Bremerhaven the shipbuilding tradition is continued and one can still have a last beer in the Kaiserhafen before leaving for New York.

Wie schon im 19. Jahrhundert machen große Passagierschiffe in Bremerhaven fest. Sie werden dort, wenn notwenig, auf der Lloydwerft repariert und gehen mit frohgelaunten Menschen wieder auf die Reise.

Large passenger boats still dock in Bremerhaven as they have done since the 19th century. They undergo repairs, if necessary, at the Lloyd Wharf and then continue their journeys with cheerful passengers.

Die Deutsche Bibliothek verzeichnet diese Publikation in der Deutschen Nationalbibliografie; detaillierte bibliografische Daten sind im Internet unter http://dnb.ddb.de abrufbar.

1. Auflage 2007

Fotos: Jochen Mönch
Text/Bildlegenden: Hermann Gutmann
Übersetzung: Hildegard and David Skevington


Hohenlohestr. 21 – 28209 Bremen
Tel. 0421-34843-0 – Fax 0421-348094
info@edition-temmen.de
www.edition-temmen.de


Gesamtherstellung: Edition Temmen
ISBN 978-3-86108-568-3